PEACE PEN PALS

HOPING FOR PEACE IN
AFGHANISTAN

Divided by conflict,
wishing for peace

Nick Hunter

raintree
a Capstone company — publishers for children

Raintree is an imprint of Capstone Global Library
Limited, a company incorporated in England and
Wales having its registered office
at 264 Banbury Road, Oxford OX2 7DY
– Registered company number: 6695582

www.raintree.co.uk
myorders@raintree.co.uk

Produced for Raintree by Calcium
Edited by Sarah Eason and John Andrews
Designed by Paul Myerscough
Picture research by Rachel Blount
Production by Victoria Fitzgerald
Originated by Capstone Global Library Ltd © 2017
Printed and bound in China

ISBN 978 1 4747 3120 1
20 19 18 17 16
10 9 8 7 6 5 4 3 2 1

**British Library Cataloguing in
Publication Data**
A full catalogue record for this book is available
from the British Library

Acknowledgements
We would like to thank the following for permission
to reproduce photographs: Dreamstime: Picstudio,
1mr, Robert Sholl, 39, Sagear, 41t, Scaramax,
31t, Thanatonautii, 4t, 12b, 12bg, 13, 28, 29bg,
Vampy1, 43m, 43bg, Venelin Petkov, 16-17t;
Image by Cpl Mike O'Neill RLC LBIPP; ©
Crown copyright 2011, 15t, Image by Neil Hall;
© Crown copyright 2011, 25t, Image by Sergeant
Ian Forsyth RLC; © Crown copyright 2011, 44b;
iStockphoto: ollo, 42; Shutterstock: Andresr, 14b,
Anton Hlushchenko, 17b, 17bg, Asianet-Pakistan,
7br, Bukhavets Mikhail, throughout, Creatista, 1ml,
Flavia Morlachetti, 1t, Ilya Andriyanov, throughout,
Jack Aiello, 24b, K2 images, 38bl, 38bg, Ken
Tannenbaum, 6l, 6bg, Larry Bruce, 6tr, Lizette
Potgieter, 9b, 21t, 36b, Monkey Business Images,
34b, Nate Derrick, 45t, Oleg Zabielin, 8, 9bg, R.
Gino Santa Maria, throughout, Ryan Rodrick Beiler,
38r, Sergey Lavrentev, throughout, SGM, 26b, SJ
Travel Photo and Video, 1m, Tom Asz, throughout,
Tracing Tea, 3, 4b, 4bg, 10b, 18b, 18bg, 41b,
Trinacria Photo, 5br; U.S. Army photo by: Spc.
Leslie Angulo, 33; U.S. Department of Defense
Photo, 5t, 20b, Cpl. Brian Gabriel Jr., 11t, Cpl. John
M. McCall, 22b, Master Sgt. Andy Dunaway, 7m,
MC2 Ernesto Hernandez Fonte, 16br, 30b, 36t,
MC2 Melissa Russell, 23m, 23bg, PH1 Ted Banks,
USN, 32t, 32bg, PO2 Aramis X. Ramirez, 26bg,
27, Sgt Albert J. Carls, 19, SPC Ian Schell, 29t,
Spc. Theodore T Schmidt, 22t; Wikimedia: Harald
Dettenborn, 37tr, 37bg

Cover art reproduced with permission of:
Dreamstime, Picstudio, bmr; Shutterstock:
Creatista, bml, Dr Flash, br, Flavia Morlachetti, t,
Gil C, bl, Nikm4860, bbg, Ryan Rodrick Beiler, tbg,
SJ Travel Photo and Video, m.

CONTENTS

WAR-TORN AFGHANISTAN

Since 2001, the United States, the United Kingdom and other countries have been involved in war in Afghanistan. Sometimes the war is headline news, but often it is not reported. For the Afghan people, however, the war never goes away. Life is always dangerous and difficult.

For the Afghan people the war began long before 2001. In fact, Afghanistan has seen almost constant conflict since the **Soviet Union** invaded the country in 1979. Sometimes Afghans have fought this conflict against forces from outside the country, but often the battles have been between different groups within Afghanistan.

Many Afghans make a living from farming in the mountainous areas that cover much of the country.

Soviet troops invaded Afghanistan in 1979 to support the Afghan **socialist** government against rebel fighters who wanted to overthrow it.

Rough land

Afghanistan is an isolated, mountainous country in central Asia. Mountains cover around three-quarters of this landlocked country, which is surrounded by other nations, including Iran and Pakistan.

Peace Pen Pals

This book looks at the war in Afghanistan through the eyes of two children on either side of the conflict. Through their letters to each other, we can learn more about what it was like to live through this terrible conflict.

AFGHANISTAN AND THE AFGHANS

Area of Afghanistan: 650,000 square kilometres (250,000 square miles) – 2.5 times bigger than the UK

Population: 31 million

Capital city: Kabul

Official languages: Dari, Pashto

Religion: 99 per cent of Afghans follow **Islam**

Afghanistan

CHAPTER ONE

THE WAR ON TERROR

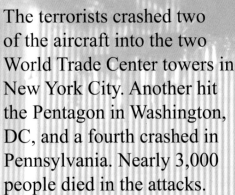

The latest war in Afghanistan began after an event that took place far away from the mountains of central Asia. On 11 September 2001, terrorists hijacked four passenger aircraft flying over the United States.

The terrorist attacks on the World Trade Center in 2001 completely destroyed the two buildings and killed thousands.

The terrorists crashed two of the aircraft into the two World Trade Center towers in New York City. Another hit the Pentagon in Washington, DC, and a fourth crashed in Pennsylvania. Nearly 3,000 people died in the attacks.

Capture or kill

US President George W. Bush vowed that terrorists who wished to attack the United States would be captured or killed in a "war on terror". The first target of this war was Osama Bin Laden. Bin Laden was believed to have ordered the attacks of 9/11, as that day became known.

The war begins

Bin Laden's al-Qaeda terrorist group was based in the remote mountains of Afghanistan. The United States demanded that the **Taliban**, which controlled much of Afghanistan, hand over Bin Laden to face trial in the United States. When the Taliban refused to give in to the demands, the **United Nations** voted to allow the use of military force in Afghanistan.

After 9/11, Bin Laden went into hiding in the remote mountain areas of Afghanistan.

OSAMA BIN LADEN

Osama Bin Laden (1957-2011) was born in Riyadh, Saudi Arabia, as the son of a wealthy businessman. He travelled to Afghanistan to help defend it against **invasion** by the Soviet Union in 1979. Bin Laden and other Arabs involved in this conflict formed al-Qaeda, a terrorist group determined to defend Muslims against foreign invasion and influence. They vowed to attack those whom they saw as the enemies of Islam.

Taliban fighters imposed the regime's harsh laws with extreme violence and brutal crackdowns on any resistance.

The Taliban in Afghanistan

In 1996, the Taliban came to power in Afghanistan. These fierce fighters were led by Mullah Mohammed Omar. They aimed to end the fighting between different groups in Afghanistan and introduce strict Islamic law across the country.

Brutal rule

At first, the Taliban was welcomed by many Afghans because it brought order to a country that was tired of many years of conflict. Although it brought peace, the brutal laws and punishments used to keep order made life worse for many people. Criminals could have body parts amputated in public, television and music were banned and men were jailed if their beards were too short. Anyone who did not follow the Taliban's strict version of Islam faced **persecution**.

Other countries condemned many of the Taliban's extreme policies. They were particularly worried about the Taliban's support for groups that planned terrorist attacks around the world, such as Osama Bin Laden's al-Qaeda.

WOMEN AND THE TALIBAN

Life under the Taliban regime was particularly difficult for women and girls. Women were forbidden to work, go to school or even leave their home without a male companion. In public, they were forced to cover their bodies from head to toe in a **burqa**. Since 2001, life has improved for the nation's women, but they still have fewer rights and freedoms compared to men in Afghan society.

Although the Taliban's harsh regime has gone, many women still wear the burqa.

RUMOURS OF WAR

Kabul, Afghanistan
September 2001
Dear Kelly,
Writing to you in the United Kingdom helps me so much with learning English. I am writing because we have heard rumours that cities in the United States have been attacked by aircraft. Some people are celebrating because they think Western countries are enemies of our government, but ordinary Afghans know better than anyone the terrible cost of war.

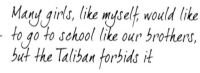

Many girls, like myself, would like to go to school like our brothers, but the Taliban forbids it

Writing in Afghanistan

The Taliban's strict ban on girls going to school means that it was unusual for girls to be able to write a letter. Only just more than 1 in 10 women in Afghanistan were able to read and write in 2000, and most had to learn secretly at home. Literacy is also a problem for Afghan men, more than half of whom cannot read and write.

Only Afghan boys went to school under Taliban rule.

We have all lost friends and relatives in the wars that have split our country for so long. We know that the victims of war are often ordinary people who want to live a peaceful life, just like the victims of the attacks in the United States.

We have no television to see what is happening in the rest of the world, but we hear rumours that forces from the United States and other countries are going to attack our country. We do not want war, but we also do not want to be loyal to the Taliban government, which treats all Afghans badly, especially women and girls.

Let us hope that our leaders can solve their disagreements without more war.

Fatimah

Invasion

The war began on 7 October 2001, when aircraft from the United States and its **allies** began bombing targets in Afghanistan. The United States and its allies planned to defeat the Taliban government with the help of Afghan forces opposed to the Taliban. They also wanted to capture Osama Bin Laden and other al-Qaeda terrorists, and destroy their bases in Afghanistan.

After a few weeks of fighting, Afghan forces captured the capital, Kabul. In December 2001, the Taliban was driven from its ruling city of Kandahar, and the government was overthrown.

Finally, it seemed as if the war might be over. However, fighting with al-Qaeda forces and remaining Taliban rebels continued in the mountains of eastern Afghanistan.

Tired of the oppressive Taliban regime, many Afghans greeted US and allied soldiers when they entered Afghanistan.

The hunt for al-Qaeda

Once the Taliban had been removed from power, allied forces concentrated on defeating al-Qaeda. Many suspected terrorists were captured and transported to a prison at the US military base in Guantanamo Bay, Cuba. But fighting in the high mountains on the border between Afghanistan and neighbouring Pakistan proved very difficult, with many of the leaders of al-Qaeda and the Taliban escaping into Pakistan.

The allied forces worked closely with Afghan locals to gather intelligence about al-Qaeda.

CIVILIAN CASUALTIES

Although the war to remove the Taliban from power lasted only a few weeks, many innocent people were caught up in the bombing and fighting for control of Afghanistan. In one incident, 65 people were killed when a US bomb hit a group of village elders.

LIVING FREELY

Bolton, England
December 2001
Dear Fatimah,
    Thanks for your letter. It seems like your life in Afghanistan is very different from ours. Like many Britons, I feel I have learnt a lot about your country since the attacks of 9/11, but your letter gave me a sense of what it's like to live with war that never seems to stop.

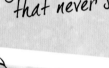

All my girlfriends have the freedom to go out and do what they want most of the time.

More troops go to war

In 2002, the US force in Afghanistan was just over 5,000 soldiers, with around 1,700 UK troops. The international force grew to include troops from more than 40 other countries. By 2010, the US forces had increased to more than 100,000 troops, with 9,500 from the UK.

My dad is serving in the British Army in Afghanistan. We all said goodbye to him a few weeks ago. He said the war would be over soon and he would be back with us. He thinks there has to be a war in Afghanistan to stop terrorists from killing people in other countries. He says the terrorists do not believe all people should have the freedom to live according to their own beliefs.

It sounds like the Taliban wasn't giving the people in your country a lot of freedom. Are you pleased that you are now getting a different government? I hope it brings peace to your country and that you'll be able to go to school just like me.

Write to me soon and tell me how things are changing in Afghanistan.

Kelly

CHAPTER TWO

AT WAR WITH THE TALIBAN

By 2003, it seemed as if the war in Afghanistan was almost over. The Taliban had been driven from power and had retreated into the mountains. The new Afghan government, led by Hamid Karzai, was preparing for elections that would give many Afghans their first chance to vote for their government.

Drug growing is a problem in Afghanistan, where local people have turned to cultivating drugs, such as opium, to make a living.

INTERNATIONAL AID

Many years of conflict have left Afghanistan one of the world's poorest countries. Most of the country's people work in agriculture, and many people are unemployed in the cities. Since 2001, the international community has sent billions of pounds of aid to Afghanistan in the hope of raising living standards. However, the continuing conflict has meant slower progress in improving life for ordinary Afghans.

All eyes on Iraq

By early 2003, the US and British armies were focused on another war, in Iraq. This gave the Taliban a chance to regroup and build up its strength in many areas of the country. It was often joined by local people who wanted to fight against the foreign forces **occupying** their country. Afghanistan's history of attempted invasions had made the people suspicious of foreign forces.

The public in the United States, the United Kingdom and other countries were also growing tired of the conflict. They had turned their attention to the war in Iraq, which was making the headlines, and many people assumed that troops in Afghanistan could now return home.

Allied forces were split between the war in Afghanistan and the new crisis in Iraq, making control of the Taliban difficult.

The Taliban fights back

In the years leading up to 2003, the Taliban had retreated to the high mountains in eastern Afghanistan and across the border to Pakistan. Its fighters were able to live beyond the reach of US and allied forces and plan the Taliban's return to power.

Gradually, the Taliban began to return to areas in the south and east of Afghanistan, where there were few US and allied forces and the government was weak and unpopular. Rather than openly attacking the allies, the Taliban fought an undercover campaign.

Local people in Afghan villages near the Taliban mountain territories became caught up in the conflict as Taliban fighters and allied forces fought bitter battles.

IEDs left by the roadside caused maiming and loss of limbs to allied soldiers and Afghan locals.

Weapons of war

The Taliban's main weapon was the **IED (Improvised Explosive Device)**. This basic bomb was often left beside a road, causing damage and injury to enemy patrols. The Taliban also used **suicide bombing** attacks, in which the bomber wears hidden explosives and is usually killed in the attack. These tactics meant that US and allied forces became bogged down in a long conflict with an almost-invisible enemy.

JOINING THE TALIBAN

Afghan fighters joined the Taliban rebels for a variety of reasons. In the countryside, the Afghan government had little control, and people saw the Taliban as a way to impose law and order. Many Taliban supporters also spoke of corruption in the new government and believed the Taliban could do a better job. In addition, the killing of friends and family during the conflict turned people against the foreign forces.

NEW FREEDOMS

Kabul, Afghanistan
February 2004
Dear Kelly,
 I'm sorry I haven't written for so long.
So much has changed with our life in Afghanistan
that I don't really know where to start.
 Life is returning to normal in Kabul after
allied and Afghan troops pushed the Taliban from
the city. We still see soldiers on our streets every
day to remind us that we are not at peace.
 It's great that girls can now go to school
again, even if we have hardly any books. We are
also able to visit the mosque, the Islamic place
of worship, and pray as normal.

Allied soldiers make an effort to get to know the local people.

Islam in Afghanistan

Almost everyone in Afghanistan follows the Islamic religion. Islamic prayer and rituals are an essential part of daily life, both in the city and countryside. Religion is one of the few aspects of life that unites the country's many **tribal** groups. Everyone in Afghanistan is expected to follow the rules of Islam, although the majority of people do not agree with the extreme religious views of groups such as the Taliban.

Women were able to pray in mosques once Taliban rule was over.

People are very excited because we're going to have elections to choose our government. It is the first time people have been able to vote for the government for 30 years. However, some people have heard that things are not so good outside of the cities. I heard my father talking about how the Taliban is taking over some villages again. I hope this doesn't mean that war will return to our streets.

Fatimah

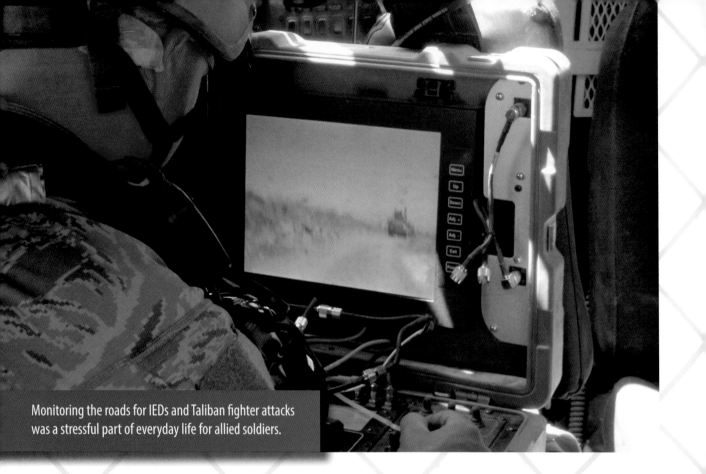

Monitoring the roads for IEDs and Taliban fighter attacks was a stressful part of everyday life for allied soldiers.

Far from home

Thousands of allied soldiers had to adjust to life in Afghanistan. Most were stationed in rural areas outside the major cities, where their fortified camps were always at risk of being attacked.

Apart from the danger of attack, one of the most difficult challenges was dealing with the Afghan **climate**. Temperatures can be incredibly high during summer but very cold in winter, particularly in the mountains. Air conditioning to deal with the heat became essential in the large tents or huts in which the soldiers lived.

Every time allied soldiers made a trip from their base they risked the deadly IEDs left by the roadside.

On patrol

Daily tasks for the soldiers included patrolling to find and **defuse** IEDs. These explosives were not just a danger for the soldiers but also for ordinary people. Although soldiers spent much of their time searching for IEDs and Taliban fighters hiding in local villages, they also helped with projects to improve life for the Afghan people.

When soldiers were off-duty, there was not much to do in rural Afghanistan. Playing cards and other games were popular ways to relax.

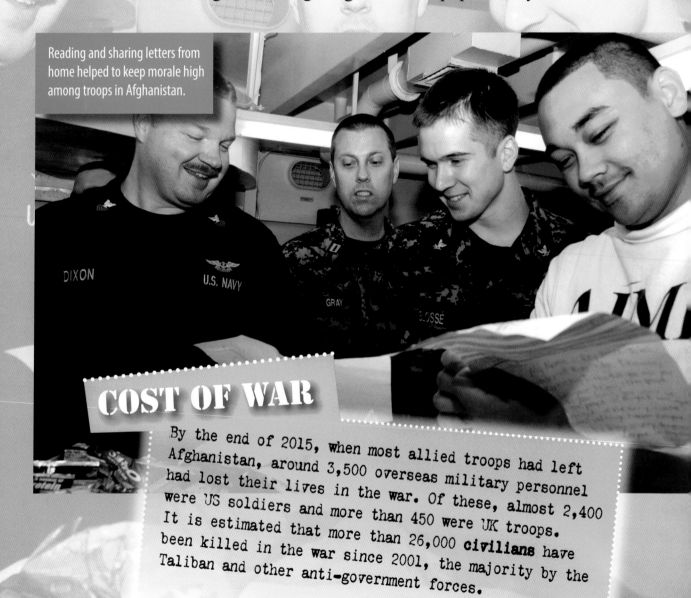

Reading and sharing letters from home helped to keep morale high among troops in Afghanistan.

DIXON
U.S. NAVY
GRAY
LOSSÉ

COST OF WAR

By the end of 2015, when most allied troops had left Afghanistan, around 3,500 overseas military personnel had lost their lives in the war. Of these, almost 2,400 were US soldiers and more than 450 were UK troops. It is estimated that more than 26,000 **civilians** have been killed in the war since 2001, the majority by the Taliban and other anti-government forces.

THOUGHTS BEFORE CHRISTMAS

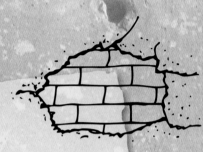

Bolton, England
December 2006
Dear Fatimah,
   I hope you are doing OK. Every day the news from Afghanistan seems to get worse. I hope none of your family or friends have been hurt in any of the bombings and other attacks that we hear about. I'm glad you're now able to go to school. I suppose that's one of the important reasons why this war is being fought.

I'm looking forward to Christmas now. It snowed here last year, but I expect it never gets as cold as Afghanistan.

Communicating with home

Use of the internet allows troops serving overseas to communicate with their families back home much more easily than in the past. Families can keep in touch by email, instant messaging and video chats, as well as with phones, letters and parcels.

We are looking forward to Christmas here. We are really lucky because Dad has come home so we are able to celebrate with him. The weather is getting cold here, and we've even had some snow. Dad says Afghanistan gets colder than England!

Every day on television we see pictures of soldiers who have been killed in the war. We don't often hear about Afghan people who have been killed, but I know thousands of your people have also died in this war.

I think we all just want this war to end, but we don't want Afghanistan to go back to how it was before the war. We just have to hope that people will find a solution.

Thinking of you and your family,

Kelly

CHAPTER THREE

LIFE DURING CONFLICT

War does not only affect the people who are fighting in it. The ordinary people of Afghanistan were just as likely to be harmed by allied air strikes or **landmines** laid by Taliban forces. These weapons killed or injured men, women and children, and they also prevented Afghans from doing essential tasks, such as planting the crops they needed for food.

Wider impact of war

As well as creating the fear of being killed or wounded, the war had an impact on many other aspects of daily life. Afghans desperately needed improvements in healthcare, education and building projects, such as roads. While the war continued, these urgent problems could not become the priority that they needed to be.

Allied forces worked hard to clear landmines from areas near Afghan villages.

Unfortunately, the troubles in Afghanistan show few signs of coming to an end. People who have endured conflict for as long as the Afghans are more likely to join armed groups to protect themselves and their families. As a result, the situation continues to be dangerous.

REFUGEES

Refugees are people who have been forced to leave their homes because of conflict or persecution. Millions of Afghan people have left the country and moved to neighbouring Pakistan and Iran. Many returned to the country after the fall of the Taliban. However, they found it extremely difficult to survive after decades of war had caused so much poverty and destruction in their homeland.

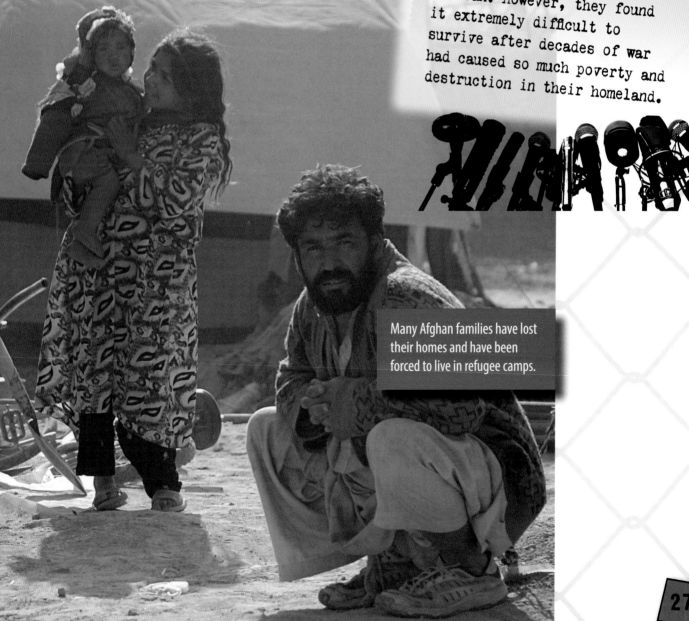

Many Afghan families have lost their homes and have been forced to live in refugee camps.

Caught up in conflict

The people of Afghanistan face many problems because of the war. Their daily lives depend on whether they live in an area controlled by Afghan government forces, or whether their area is under Taliban control. Many areas are fought over by both sides.

The capital, Kabul, was once a beautiful city, but years of war have shattered many of its buildings. Although the city remains in government control, it has also suffered from suicide bombings and other Taliban attacks, making daily life there extremely dangerous and stressful for ordinary citizens.

Living with tanks and soldiers on the streets became part of daily life for local people in the devastated city of Kabul.

Sniffer dogs are used to help search for and clear areas of mines. Mine clearance is now an important part of stabilizing life for local Afghans.

Living with danger

Most Afghans live outside the cities and work as farmers, but the country's dry climate and frequent **droughts** make it difficult to grow enough food. Landmines and IEDs have made life outside the cities dangerous, too. In addition, many of the villages in the south and east of the country are controlled by the Taliban. Afghans have to cooperate with the Taliban but often face patrols and searches from government forces.

THE DRUG TRADE

One of Afghanistan's main crops is the poppy. This flower is used to produce heroin and other illegal drugs transported to countries around the world. During Taliban rule, the poppy trade from Afghanistan decreased, but it has increased again since the war began. In Taliban-controlled areas, selling poppies for the drug trade helps the Taliban to fund its war.

DIFFICULT TIMES

Kabul, Afghanistan
15 September 2007
Dear Kelly,
    I hope that you are well and that your father
has returned safely to the United States, although
I think there are more soldiers in Afghanistan than
ever before. Life has been very difficult here, and
the peace we hope for seems a long way away.

Allied forces often
evacuated villages to clear
mines left by the Taliban.

Resisting the Taliban

Although the Taliban has received some support in the countryside, there is fear of its return in the cities. Many people, especially women, are unwilling to go back to the Taliban's harsh rule, even if it brings an end to suicide bombings and other Taliban attacks.

We fear Taliban attacks.

Almost every day, we hear news of bombings or attacks around the country. Suicide bombings are common, even in Kabul. It is too dangerous to go out unless we really have to. Some people in Kabul have become rich from the war, but many people struggle to feed their families.

We are now angry with all sides in this war. Our government and the international forces are not able to protect us from the Taliban's bombers.

The only peace that most people can remember was the terrible time when the Taliban ruled Afghanistan. I love my family, and the people of my country, but I am thinking it must be better to live in peace away from Afghanistan than stay here with this constant war.

Maybe I will come and meet you in England one day.

Fatimah

Many soldiers saw friends and colleagues killed or injured. Explaining their experiences with friends and family back home was an essential way of dealing with the difficulties they faced in the war.

Waiting at home

In the late 2000s, as the war dragged on and more young soldiers were killed, the public in the many countries involved began to turn against the war. Surveys found that US and UK citizens were only narrowly in favour of keeping troops in Afghanistan until the war could be completed. However, the public continued to support the soldiers themselves and hoped that a new US president, backed by his allies, would be able to end the war.

Within a few weeks of taking power in 2009, President Barack Obama sent thousands more US troops to Afghanistan. Their mission was to protect the Afghan people from attack from the Taliban and weaken its hold on the country.

Effects on families

The surge in troops meant that there were even more families waiting for loved ones to return from the war. Since 2001, 2.7 million US and more than 200,000 UK military personnel have served overseas in Afghanistan and Iraq. The number of family members affected by the war has been even greater, with one parent having to look after children alone, and children suffering from having an absent parent.

As more soldiers were sent to Afghanistan, the number of casualties also rose.

EFFECTS OF WAR ON SOLDIERS

The experience of fighting in a war and being in constant danger can also change the people who do the fighting. Once they return home, military personnel have to deal with the lasting effects of these stresses, which can be very difficult for them and their families.

A FORGOTTEN WAR?

Bolton, England
January 2008
Dear Fatimah,

It was very difficult to read your last letter. This war has been going on so long and it's heartbreaking to think that things are actually getting worse for you.

Most of the girls in my class could not imagine living in a place where they could not leave their home to study or work.

Schools in Afghanistan

In 2001, only around 1 million children attended school in Afghanistan, and almost all of them were boys. In 2015, the Afghan government estimated that 8.4 million children were attending school, 39 per cent of them girls. This growth in the number of students attending school has continued in spite of attacks on schools by the Taliban.

Although we don't have to cope with the dangers of living in a war zone, it is difficult to be cheerful at the moment. We miss Dad so much, but we are much luckier than those families whose loved ones will not be coming home at all.

It feels strange at school because most of the kids don't really think about the war. It has been going on for so long, some people can't remember that our troops were sent there to stop more terrorist attacks. I'm sure if people knew more about the people of Afghanistan, they would understand why we are fighting the Taliban.

I hope things will start getting better soon.

Kelly

CHAPTER FOUR

HOPES FOR PEACE

When Barack Obama became US President, the war against the Taliban had been raging for more than seven years. After the successes of 2001 and 2002, few people believed the war would last so long. However, the history of conflict in Afghanistan shows that wars are rarely over quickly in that country.

Afghan soldiers have now taken over the fight against the Taliban and hope to maintain peace in the country.

Pushing out the Taliban

In December 2009, President Obama announced that a further 30,000 US troops would be sent to Afghanistan. With more troops, the United States hoped to push Taliban fighters out of the areas they controlled.

More troops attacking the Taliban meant that the number of allied soldiers killed and wounded went up. This led to more US and UK citizens calling for an end to the war.

When will it end?

At the same time as troop numbers surged, the two sides of the conflict started to talk about agreeing to an end. This would not be easy, but many people believe that neither side can win a total victory.

Afghan leader Hamid Karzai had the job of leading his country out of war and into future peace.

WHO ARE THE TALIBAN?

The forces fighting the government and international forces in Afghanistan are usually called the Taliban. Most continue to follow its extreme form of Islam set up by Mullah Omar, who was killed in 2013. However, not all Afghans fighting on the Taliban's side are hard-line Taliban followers. Many have other reasons for fighting, such as the loss of friends or relatives in the conflict.

A changing conflict

By 2011, thousands of soldiers were fighting in the country. In June of that year, President Obama announced that many troops would return home the following year. He said the United States had succeeded in stopping al-Qaeda and killed its leaders, including Osama Bin Laden (see page 42).

President Obama found himself under increasing pressure to bring home US troops from Afghanistan.

Britain, France and other countries were also keen to bring their soldiers home. But who would take over from them?

Afghan forces

The Afghan army had always played a big part in the conflict, so an agreement was reached between the Afghan government and the allied forces to hand over command of the war to the Afghans. From 2012, US and UK soldiers began to focus on training and supporting the Afghan army. The process was not easy. While many Afghans increasingly resented foreign soldiers on their land, others worried whether the Afghan army could protect them.

Afghan forces patrol the mountain areas of their country. Many Afghan people are not confident that soldiers such as these will protect them properly, since some have been found to be working for the Taliban.

DRONE ATTACKS

US forces increased their use of Unmanned Aerial Vehicles (UAVs), or **drones**, to launch missile attacks against enemies. These planes are piloted by remote control. They can hit difficult targets without putting a pilot in danger. However, Taliban fighters do not wear uniforms, so those who operated the drones had to be sure that they did not attack civilians by mistake.

Kabul, Afghanistan
20 October 2010
Dear Kelly,

There is so much that is dangerous or does not work as it should in this country, but I suppose we must celebrate what we have achieved

In September, I voted for the first time in an election for parliament, the lawmaking body of our government All 18-year-olds are allowed to vote, although we ran the risk of being caught in a bomb or rocket attack Many Afghans said that the election was unfair and that some people voted more than once. But ten years ago, we did not dare dream of any election

I can hardly remember what it was like for girls when the Taliban was in Kabul. We are now free to leave the house and go to school, although suicide bombings make it very dangerous..

I think I would like to become a teacher one day I dream of teaching my class in a garden, with no bombs or gunfire to be heard in a peaceful country

I will tell my students about the British girl who wrote to me, and who wanted peace just like me.

Fatimah

Government changeover

Hamid Karzai was elected as Afghanistan's president in 2004 and in 2009. Ashraf Ghani won the 2014 election and was confirmed as president in September 2014. He immediately signed a security agreement with the United States and its allies for 13,000 international support troops to remain in Afghanistan after fighting troops left in December 2014.

Despite the difficulties that still exist in Afghanistan, girls like myself can now go to school, and women have been helped to set up their own businesses. I hope these good things last!

#Osama bin Laden was shot in the head, congressional source says
http://on.cnn.com/k6b6tS - @cnnbrk

011 – Updated 0913 GMT (1713 HKT)

LATEST

OSAMA BIN LADEN DEAD

lusive al Qaeda
ounder killed,
buried at sea

Osama bin Laden, al Qaeda founder and
astermind of the 9/11 terror attacks, is
buried at sea after he is killed in an
operation by U.S. forces in Pakistan,
officials say. FULL STORY

The death of Osama Bin Laden made news headlines around the world. However, the Taliban still poses a great threat.

Finding Bin Laden

In 2011, the United States finally achieved one of its main goals in the war – hunting down the terrorist leader Osama Bin Laden. He had evaded capture for almost 10 years. US forces knew he was still alive because he produced audio and video recordings encouraging his supporters to attack his enemies.

In August 2010, US intelligence officials detected a phone call from one of Bin Laden's closest supporters. They tracked him to a **compound** in a small Pakistani town. On 2 May 2011, a team of US **special forces** travelled by helicopter from Afghanistan and raided the compound. There they shot and killed Bin Laden.

No peace yet ...

The death of Bin Laden pleased the British public, but it brought little hope for peace in Afghanistan. The Afghan people have been losing trust in their government and suspect it of being corrupt.

The Taliban has gained new recruits and continues to wage war against the Afghan army and explode bombs across the country. The Taliban is taking control of more towns and villages. In 2016, 40 per cent of young Afghans wanted to emigrate.

The success of the US military mission to find and kill Bin Laden has not wiped out the danger al-Qaeda poses, but it has weakened the organization.

PAKISTAN QUESTION

The Taliban has had a strong link with Pakistan for a long time. Many of its schools, or madrasas, are there. At the same time, Pakistan is an ally of the United States in its war on terror and has suffered many attacks as a result. However, Pakistani military and intelligence officers have been suspected of helping the Taliban and may even have known where Bin Laden was hiding.

HOME AGAIN!

Bolton, England
November 2014
Dear Fatimah,
    I am so excited We heard a few weeks ago that my dad would be coming back from Afghanistan in time for Christmas. He is back now and it has been great having our whole family together for the holiday.
    We know how lucky we are. Many soldiers are staying in Afghanistan to train and support your army. We also know that, for you and other Afghans, the war is still going on. At least I now know a bit about your country and what life is like for you.

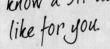

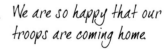

We are so happy that our troops are coming home.

Reasons for hope

Although the continuing conflict is the biggest concern for the people in Afghanistan, there are some reasons to be optimistic about the future.

The average Afghan has more money today compared to 2001. Most people are not rich, but products and services that Westerners take for granted, such as healthcare and mobile phones, are more widespread.

If the Taliban can make a peace agreement with the Afghan government, many of the people who have left the country might return, but only if that peace treaty secures basic human rights for everyone.

We have hope for the future!

I would like to visit your country someday. The ordinary people of Afghanistan are so brave, and the mountains must be so beautiful. When you are a teacher, I could come and talk to your class about the friend who helped me to learn all about your wonderful country. I will keep hoping for peace so your wishes can come true.

Your friend,

GLOSSARY

ally nation that is on the same side as another in a conflict

burqa garment that covers the head and face, worn by some Muslim women

civilian person who is not a member of the military services

climate weather patterns of a particular region

compound enclosed area in which one or more houses or buildings stand

defuse make a bomb or other kind of explosive safe

drone unmanned remote-controlled aircraft

drought long span of time with little or no rain

IED (Improvised Explosive Device) home-made bomb left on roadsides, used as a weapon by Taliban fighters in Afghanistan

invasion takeover of a place or country, usually by military force

Islam religion based on the teachings of the prophet Muhammad

landmine bomb that is buried in the ground and explodes when stepped on

occupy to take control of a space or country for a period of time

persecution harsh and unfair treatment of a person or group

refugee person who is forced to leave home because of war or persecution

socialist one who believes in perfect equality among people

Soviet Union group of countries, including present-day Russia, that existed as a single nation between 1922 and 1991

special force military unit that carries out particularly skilled or dangerous missions

suicide bombing bomb attack in which the bomb is carried by the bomber, who usually dies in the explosion

Taliban Islamic militant and political group that held power in Afghanistan between 1996 and 2001 and which continues to fight against Afghan government forces

terrorist person or group that carries out acts of violence against civilians to achieve a political goal

tribal relating to a tribe or group linked by family ties and culture

United Nations international organization that includes representatives of most countries in the world, and which rules in cases of international disputes

FIND OUT MORE

Books

Afghanistan (Countries Around the World), Jovanka J. Milivojevic (Raintree, 2012)

Razia's Ray of Hope: One Girl's Dream of an Education, Elizabeth Suneby (Wayland, 2015)

The Hunt for Bin Laden (Cornerstones of Freedom), Josh Gregory (Scholastic, 2013)

War in Afghanistan and Iraq: The Daily Life of the Men and Women Serving in Afghanistan and Iraq, Gerry Souter and Janet Souter (Carlton, 2011)

Websites

Discover the history of the Afghanistan war and watch video features on life for families in that country:
www.bbc.co.uk/newsround/15214375

Learn how the United Kingdom is involved in Afghanistan:
www.gov.uk/government/publications/uks-work-in-afghanistan/ the-uks-work-in-afghanistan

Visit this online gallery, which shows pictures of children's lives in Afghanistan:
news.bbc.co.uk/cbbcnews/hi/pictures/galleries/newsid_1792000/1792337.stm

See what the War Child charity does for children in Afghanistan and learn about the country and its history:
www.warchild.org.uk/issues/war-afghanistan

INDEX